MASTERS OF WORLD PAINTING

Paul Cézanne

HARRY N. ABRAMS, INC., PUBLISHERS, NEW YORK
AURORA ART PUBLISHERS, LENINGRAD

COMPILED AND INTRODUCED BY YEKATERINA DREVINA
TRANSLATED FROM THE RUSSIAN BY HELEN KLIER
DESIGNED BY VIACHESLAV BAKHTIN

Library of Congress Catalog Card Number: 81-67168
International Standard Book Number: 0-8109-2251-7

© 1981 by Aurora Art Publishers, Leningrad

Created by Aurora Art Publishers, Leningrad,
for joint publication of Aurora and Harry N. Abrams, Inc., New York

PRINTED AND BOUND IN THE USSR

It is difficult to overestimate Cézanne's impact on later generations of artists. All of the most important masters of the first half of the twentieth century were indebted to him for their own innovations in art. Matisse once said, "Cézanne is our father." Any major trend in modern painting, whether Fauvism, Cubism, or Expressionism, grew out of Cézanne's achievements in the treatment of space, use of color, the construction of composition, and free portrayal of objects.

Camille Pissarro, a friend of Cézanne's, wrote: "Curiously enough, while I was admiring this strange, disconcerting aspect of Cézanne, familiar to me for many years, Renoir arrived. But my enthusiasm was nothing compared to Renoir's. Degas himself is seduced by the charm of this refined savage, Monet, all of us. . . . Are we mistaken? I don't think so. The only ones who are not subject to the charm of Cézanne are precisely those artists or collectors who have shown by their errors that their sensibilities are defective."

This letter of Pissarro's was written on the eve of the twentieth century, in 1895, when a young art dealer, Ambroise Vollard, inspired by all the growing interest in the artist from Provence, organized an exhibition of Cézanne's fifty-eight paintings in a small gallery on Rue Laffitte in Paris.

Cézanne's genius was also recognized by the well-known Russian collectors Ivan Morozov and Sergei Shchukin, who bought between them twenty-six of his canvases at the beginning of the century, including those that had no versions or replicas in other collections. Thus *Girl at the Piano. Overture to Tannhäuser* (1868—69, The Hermitage, Leningrad; Plate 2) is the only extant variant of this composition, since two other works on the theme, known from recollections by contemporaries, were destroyed by the artist. Similarly, there are no analogues to *Pierrot and Harlequin. Mardi Gras* (1888, The Pushkin Museum of Fine Arts, Moscow; Plate 7), the acknowledged masterpiece of the mature Cézanne, which was bought, apparently, during his lifetime. It can thus be said that Soviet museums possess Cézanne's first-rate works

covering the basic stages of his career and providing a fairly complete picture of his artistic development.

Cézanne's œuvre is usually divided into four periods: romantic, Impressionist, analytical (constructivist), and synthetic. This classification, albeit conditional, on the whole accurately reflects the characteristic changes his works underwent with the passage of time. The exact definition of the limits of each period is especially important, because in most cases this has been the only way to establish the date of one painting or another, since the artist rarely dated them. However, this is a much-disputed problem, and in monographs about Cézanne art historians differ widely in assessing the dates of his compositions. Therefore we will discuss his works in ten-year periods, beginning in the 1860s.

Paul Cézanne was born in 1839 into the family of a wealthy banker in Aix-en-Provence, an old provincial town in the south of France. Here he spent most of his life and produced his best works. From 1862 on, Cézanne often went to Paris. He had the firm intention of becoming an artist, but before making up his mind, he hesitated for a long time, doubting whether this would be the right choice. A man with a powerful artistic temperament and an unusually sensitive perception of life, he felt the profound disparity between his own view of the world and the generally accepted standards that predominated in art. The desire to translate this vision into reality steadily drew him to his true vocation.

In Paris, Cézanne frequented the Académie Suisse, an academy by name only, but in actual fact a common studio, where, for a fee, any beginner could receive some professional advice and the opportunity to work from the nude. However, even then, during his apprenticeship, Cézanne did not aim toward an exact reproduction of the model; instead, he boldly distorted the proportions of the figures and created bizarre images.

Every morning without fail Cézanne set off for the Académie Suisse and worked there at length for several hours. His real teachers, however, were the Old Masters, whom he often copied in the Louvre.

He particularly admired the sixteenth-century Venetian masters, above all the dramatically expressive art of Tintoretto. He himself produced numerous compositions, such as *The Judgment of Paris, The Temptation of St. Anthony,* and *Déjeuner sur l'herbe,* where a free treatment of form is not restrained by any rules of proportion and spatial relationships.

This period of Cézanne's artistic career is represented in Soviet museums only by the painting *Two Women and Child in an Interior* (early 1860s, The Pushkin Museum of Fine Arts, Moscow; Plate 1), a picture that affords just a glimpse into his early efforts but that nevertheless clearly shows how freely he treated the human figure to achieve greater expression. The heightened expression characteristic of this everyday family-life scene hallmarked many of Cézanne's early works. It is not by chance that most researchers have grown accustomed to calling this period "romantic" or "baroque." Despite all the originality of its plastic form, the painting still evokes associations with works by the Old Masters, although, unlike them, it generates the feeling of inner tension.

The girl and two ladies in colorful crinoline dresses, grouped around a table on which stands a bowl of goldfish, are painted with dense, thick brushstrokes. Their looks and gestures are directed to the center. The bright patch of the girl's figure bursts into the darkness, interrupting the smooth movement of the woman's hands. However, the dynamic turn of the girl's figure is so balanced that this simple genre motif acquires some uncertain but profound meaning. Thanks to the powerful, seemingly protruding volumes, the composition calls to mind a bright relief on the dark, almost black surface.

The Old Masters were not the only source of Cézanne's inspiration; modern artists also attracted him, above all Gustave Courbet and Édouard Manet.

At the end of the 1860s, Cézanne started to use a more restrained and strict composition. Alongside baroque and romantic works, he painted his *Girl at the Piano* in which he once again turned to the interior motif, depicting the drawing room at the Jas de Bouffan, his family's estate. The horizontal and vertical elements give the composition a classical severity that probably betrays the influence of Manet's *Madame Manet at the Piano* (c. 1867, Musée de l'Impressionnisme, Paris), which Cézanne might have seen. In a desire to suppress his predilection for rendering volumes as if in relief, the artist flattened the figures, accentuating them with dark outlines and designating the surrounding space by the folds of the carpet and the keyboard of the piano receding into the depths of the canvas. *Girl at the Piano* epitomizes those compositional devices that were to distinguish Cézanne's artistic method in the years to come.

In *Girl at the Piano* there are no traditional signs of the interior scene: the room of the country house is transformed by the artist's brush into an enclosed world, a compact space saturated with dense splashes of color that has to be contemplated with concentration. This painting is reminiscent of Wagner's music, which demands a similar mental effort on the part of the listener. It is not accidental that the picture has the subtitle *Overture to Tannhäuser*, and as such is a tribute to Wagner, whose opera was hostilely received by the general public in Paris, while the young generation of artists, including Cézanne, regarded it with full understanding and sympathy as a revolutionary breakthrough in music.

In the 1860s, Cézanne's work bears the character of an intense, passionate, at times agonizing search. He felt the keen necessity of discipline and clearly realized the need to move from the studio out-of-doors. In this respect he had predecessors — a group of young artists, many of whom he knew well or befriended — Monet, Pissarro, and Renoir, who had already painted a long while *en plein air.*

From 1872, Cézanne lived in Pontoise and Auvers-sur-Oise, where he worked with Pissarro. They often painted the same subjects — for instance, the view of the road at Pontoise (*Road at Pontoise.* 1878, The Pushkin Museum of Fine Arts, Moscow; Plate 3). However, it would be too simple to explain the difference in treatment of one and the same landscape by the artists' temperaments alone, for the difference went much deeper. Pissarro, like the majority of Impressionists, rejoiced in the sun, streaming light, and flowing water, and aimed to depict only a small corner of nature. But Cézanne strove to reflect the world in its entirety. Nonetheless, from the viewpoint of the painterly technique, Cézanne's work during this period came closest to Impressionism. Truth to say, Pissarro played no small part in this development.

Cézanne's palette lightened, and he began to apply finer strokes, using much less frequently the knife and spatula, formerly his indispensable tools. Yet, even in such a work as *Vase of Flowers* (1873—75, The Hermitage, Leningrad), executed in the Impressionist manner, the artist still focused on conveying the material structure of the visible world. His dense strokes resemble clots of pigment that preserve their viscosity on the textured surface of the canvas.

Self-Portrait in a Casquette. 1873—75
Oil on canvas. $20^3/_4 \times 14^1/_8''$ (53 $\times$ 38 cm)
The Hermitage, Leningrad

Plain by Mont Sainte-Victoire. 1882 — 85
Oil on canvas. 22⁷/₈ × 28¹/₄″ (58 × 72 cm)
The Pushkin Museum of Fine Arts, Moscow

Self-Portrait in a Casquette (1873—75, The Hermitage, Leningrad), done at the same time as *Vase of Flowers*, is striking for its sculptural qualities in comparison with the portraits by most Impressionists. Although the facial features are well-delineated, the representation is not free from superfluous elements. If we compare this portrait with the *Self-Portrait* in the Pushkin Museum of Fine Arts in Moscow (1879 — 85; Plate 4), we can trace the changes in the artist's approach toward his models and their form. A powerful plasticity in the rendition of volume in the latter portrait is achieved not by the customary light-and-shade modeling but by the colored modulations of yellow and green, the most subtle combinations of warm and cold tones. Cézanne's manner is more precise, the color

scale more restrained, yet richer. The plastic modeling and the sharp strokes combine to reveal the painter's inner man, the workings of his creative mind.

During the exhibitions of 1874 and 1877, Cézanne and the Impressionists joined together in the struggle against their common adversaries: the Académie, its jury, and the official Salons, which stubbornly clung to the outmoded, routine forms in art. But already in the 1880s, their views widely diverged, particularly as concerned landscape painting, a genre most fully developed by the Impressionists.

At first glance it seems as if there were no essential difference in their approach to the object depicted. Just like Claude Monet and Pissarro, Cézanne always painted from life in the open air. Creating cycles of

The Banks of the Marne (Villa on the Bank of a River). 1888
Oil on canvas. 25⅝ × 31⅞" (65 × 81 cm)
The Hermitage, Leningrad

pictures on the same motif, he thoroughly studied the character of light reflections and the contrasts of warm and cold tones of color. However, the aims pursued by Cézanne and the Impressionists were of a quite different order. In his *Haystacks* and *Poplars* Monet primarily tried to capture on canvas the instantaneous, fleeting states of nature, focusing on changing effects of light and air. Cézanne, on the other hand, sought to reveal the immanent states independent of the time of day, illumination, and so forth. He never treated his motifs in the same way; painting a landscape, the artist would choose the vantage point best suited for presenting a given locality and depicted the same view from different angles. This approach is exemplified by *Plain by Mont Sainte-Victoire* (1882—85, The Push-

kin Museum of Fine Arts, Moscow) and *Mont Sainte-Victoire* (1882—85, The Barnes Foundation, Merion).

In the first picture, the mountain massif is cut off on both sides of the canvas, implying that the composition extends beyond the limits of the frame. Owing to the flat valley in the middle part of the canvas, the landscape looks like a kind of strip between earth and sky, although the planes are distinctly bounded. The picture in the Barnes Foundation appears to be better constructed. The vantage point chosen here is the road that runs diagonally from the center to the clear-cut horizontal line designating the foot of the mountain, and it imparts to the scene greater stability. Such devices undoubtedly enabled the artist to correlate more precisely all the elements of a landscape painting.

7

Cézanne continued to develop this technique in his cycle of views of Mont Sainte-Victoire from the side of Montbriant in Bellevue, where his sister's estate was situated and where he worked from 1885 to 1887. This is best illustrated by two depictions of *Mont Sainte-Victoire with a Great Pine* in the Phillips Collection in Washington D. C., and the Courtauld Institute in London. Once again these are companion paintings in which the same motif is presented from different vantage points, a principle Cézanne adhered to in the mid-1880s, his so-called "constructivist" period. Views of the Sainte-Victoire from the side of Montbriant bear an essentially experimental character in that they reflect the artist's study of the motif, his treatment of spatial planes, which at the time he still perceived as a combination of isolated elements. In *Pierrot and Harlequin. Mardi Gras*, the most important work in Soviet collections, the artist has already achieved a complex spatial balance of the figures that manage to preserve stability while walking on an inclined plane.

The Aqueduct (1885 — 87, The Pushkin Museum of Fine Arts, Moscow; Plate 5) is also related to the *Mont Sainte-Victoire* cycle in that it depicts the same Arc Valley and the same mountain visible through the crowns of the trees.

At the end of the 1880s, Cézanne's researches aimed at optimally coordinating spatial zones in a landscape reached their final phase, a phase usually regarded as the transition from the analytical to the synthetic period. This transition is manifest in a group of canvases depicting the banks of the Marne, two of the best of which belong to Soviet collections.

The Banks of the Marne (c. 1888, The Pushkin Museum of Fine Arts, Moscow; Plate 6) is one of Cézanne's masterpieces, notable for its generalized forms filling the deep space of the picture. The various planes are interconnected by the reflection of the landscape in the crystal-clear water. The only thing dividing them is the narrow strip of bank that seemingly recedes into the distance but in actual fact terminates on the central pier of the bridge. This work serves to illustrate Cézanne's first efforts at solving the problem of perceptual perspective.

In *The Banks of the Marne* (*Villa on the Bank of a River*), a picture of 1888 in the Hermitage collection, the artist separates the expanse of the river and the greenery surrounding the white building by the intermittent line of the bank, now lost amidst the greenery, now sinking into the water and merging with the reflections. The blue-green color scale unites everything — water, trees, sky — showing features of the

color equilibrium that generally distinguished Cézanne's canvases in the 1890s.

Cézanne gradually arrived at his system of perspective, changing ideas that had never been challenged before by his most progressive-minded contemporaries. He found objective criteria within nature for the correlation of forms in space and it is partly for this reason that time and again he turned to the still-life genre. He consistently resolved the problem of bringing out the relationships of spatial forms by first arranging objects on a table and then transferring the volumes and the relationships thus obtained onto the canvas.

Louis Le Bail, who once saw how painstakingly Cézanne arranged a still life, later recalled: "The cloth was very slightly draped upon the table, with innate taste. Then Cézanne arranged the fruits, contrasting the tones one against the other, making the complementaries vibrate. . . . tipping, turning, balancing the fruits as he wanted them to be, using one or two sous for the purpose. He brought to this task the greatest care and many precautions; one guessed that it was a feast for the eye to him."

The same objects, usually a jug, sugarbowl, and table populate his still lifes alongside peaches, pears, apples, and oranges. The artist sought to achieve the maximum of generalization in each individual form, to convey in it the qualities inherent in one particular type. He discarded everything superfluous and transient, everything that stood in the way of integral perception (*Peaches and Pears.* 1888 — 90, The Pushkin Museum of Fine Arts, Moscow; Plate 8).

The massive, rounded fruits in the *Still Life with Curtain* (1899, The Hermitage, Leningrad; Plate 12) seem to slide down the sloping surface of the table and hang onto it thanks only to their own weight. The cloths are about to slip off the edge of the table but become frozen in the immobility of their folds. On the other hand, the frontally depicted planes of the curtain and the jug stress the stability of the physical world. However, the static quality of the articles is at once disturbed by the curving lines of their ornament. The background loses the significance of a backdrop, changing into condensed streams of air. There arises the feeling of a constantly mobile and, at the same time, eternally existing world of nature. The brushstrokes are remarkably flexible and plastic, molding form and marking off space. They seem to be clinging to one another, thereby forming an indissoluble structure of the painting.

For Cézanne, man is an integral part of Nature, governed by its immutable laws, a fundamental concept embodied in his compositions of bathers. In his *Bathers* (early 1890s, The Pushkin Museum of Fine Arts, Moscow; Plate 9), the human figures and nature are not opposed to each other, but are perceived as a single spatial entity. The nude youths are pierced by the blue air, as it were, their motions free and natural, while the position of their figures is subordinated to a well-thought-out plastic rhythm. The study is one of the many variants of the motif which Cézanne used more than once and which found its expression in the artist's later works. In these canvases he embodied his ideal of a free, unfettered life amidst nature, an ideal that evolved in his imagination during his youth when he, together with Émile Zola and Baptistin Baille, spent days by the river Arc in the neighborhood of Aix.

Cézanne's aim in his *Bathers* was of a quite different order than that pursued by the Impressionists, who endeavored to show the nude figure in a variety of states; suffice it to recall Degas's brilliant series of nudes. Cézanne, on the other hand, strove to lend the ordinary motif of bathing a tinge of classical sublimity.

In recollections of his happy youth there loomed the persistent image of a tall pine in the Arc Valley. One of its representations is the *Great Pine near Aix* (late 1890s, The Hermitage, Leningrad; Plate 10). The powerful curving branches of the tree and its stalwart trunk produce the sensation of security. All the elements around the tree — the air and earth, light and shade — create a mobile mass of freely flowing color patches. This is the way Cézanne solves the problem of integrating the object with the space surrounding it. He unfolds space using the tree branches as reference points. Together with the trunk they create that spatial grid that accounts for the unity and tension of the composition. Applying planes of yellow, green, blue, and orange, one upon the other, the artist virtually molds a relief of the area. The unity of the planes thus achieved was the salient feature of his landscapes painted in the late 1890s and early 1900s.

Striving to find a balance between the dynamic and the static determined Cézanne's work on figure compositions. He painstakingly chose the pose of his models, tiring them with an endless number of sittings. The artist did not impart individual characteristics to his models, nor did he recount their lives or convey their moods, but created instead a generalized, profound image of the human being. Such is his *Smoker* (1895 — 1900, The Hermitage, Leningrad; Plate 11), massive and monumental, carved out of a solid block of stone, as it were. Such, too, is the *Lady in Blue* (1904, The Hermitage, Leningrad; Plate 14), whose

palpable feebleness can be sensed in the pointed and angular forms of her figure and costume.

In his later works, Cézanne no longer attempted to subordinate the composition to a certain scheme conceived in his mind's eye. This scheme arose by itself as the direct offshoot of his understanding of a picture. It was toward the beginning of this century that the lyrical intonation started to prevail in his works (*Old Woman with Rosaries*, 1900—4, National Gallery, London; *Youth in a Red Waistcoat*, early 1900s, watercolor, private collection, Zurich; *Portrait of the Gardener Vallier*, 1904—6; watercolor, private collection, Los Angeles). In that period Cézanne practically never left Aix, finding an inexhaustible fount of inspiration in the nature of Provence, and Mont Sainte-Victoire in particular.

Never before did Cézanne endow this motif with such a sense of majesty and grandeur, such a feeling of the unity and wholeness of the universe. In *Mont Sainte-Victoire*, painted in 1896—98 (The Hermitage, Leningrad; Plate 13), the mountain seems to be woven out of streams of cold air. The vigorous outline designates its peak, separating it from the sky. The artist, greatly increasing the dimensions of the mountain in relation to the adjacent hollows and tracts of forest, brings it closer to the viewer while preserving the impression of its inaccessibility. Thus the traveler looking at a mountaintop thinks that it is quite near, but making for it he sees at once that it does not seem to come any nearer, teasing him by its sham proximity.

Cézanne's colors are more intense, although the color scale is more restricted. By merely contrasting greens and reddish-yellows, he creates the sensation of bright vegetation and reddish earth. The same shades serve to convey the three-dimensionality of forms that always resemble simple geometric figures— the cone, the sphere, and the cylinder.

In all his works done in the 1900s, Cézanne invariably realized his sensations of space and form through color. Often dissatisfied, he gave up one canvas about halfway through to start on another. Today these so-called unfinished works strike us with their artistry and logical construction.

The Blue Landscape (1904 — 6, The Hermitage, Leningrad; Plate 15)—one of the masterpieces of this period—captivates the onlooker by its rich, saturated colors and unrestrained brushwork. The artist needs no linear means to build up the picture. He creates space by the curving strokes of his brush skimming over the canvas's surface. Although intense and multilayered, the color retains its lightness. Next to the bright splashes of deep blue, green, and yellow is the surface of unpainted priming. Especially light, compared to the glaring green in the foreground, is the distant landscape pierced by the blue highlights that help create a color equilibrium.

Views of the Sainte-Victoire from the hills of Les Lauves, where Cézanne built his studio in 1902, comprise the most important series of canvases depicting this mountain. One of these, *Landscape at Aix* (*Mont Sainte-Victoire*), dated 1905—6, is in the Pushkin Museum of Fine Arts in Moscow (Plate 16).

The Sainte-Victoire has a nearly conical form, and the center of the cone is markedly shifted to the right. A comparison of this depiction with the photograph taken by John Rewald shows that the artist followed the outlines dictated by the locality, but he strongly generalized all the elements of the landscape and sharpened the form of the mountain. Thanks to the alternation of green and warm yellow tones changing into blues, the picture is perceived as a single whole.

Much has been said about the "incompleteness" of Cézanne's later landscapes, including the cycle just mentioned. This incompleteness as an artistic method is characteristic of his entire late period. It is noteworthy that in the course of time, more and more of Cézanne's paintings have been classified as finished, although his contemporaries, and even such admirers as Émile Bernard, regarded only ten or fifteen works by the master as fully completed.

In his landscapes of the 1900s, the artist sought to convey all the diversity and wealth of nature by means of accurate color relationships. As soon as the problem of spatial relationships expressed by color was resolved, the artist ceased to work on the picture.

At the sunset of his life Cézanne was obsessed with the thought that he would no longer be able to feel nature and create art in conversation with it. One week before his death, he wrote to his son: "Sketches, pictures, if I were to do any, would be merely constructions after nature, based on method, sensations, and developments suggested by the model...."

Cézanne's work is a shining example of tireless quests for novel and more perfect means of expression, which, as Maurice Denis aptly observed, he was forced to invent as his eye and mind demanded.

Cézanne's art, like the bud of a plant, contained, as it were, the genetic code of the evolution of all European painting in the twentieth century. It gave birth to a plethora of followers who continued to develop the great artist's achievements.

BIOGRAPHICAL OUTLINE

1839 Born on January 19, in Aix-en-Provence, into the family of Louis-Auguste Cézanne, a factory owner and banker, and Elizabeth Auber, daughter of a woodcarver

1852—58 Studies at the Collège Bourbon in Aix. Receives his baccalaureate on November 12, 1858. In 1856 begins to attend the drawing courses of Joseph-Marc Gibert at the Ecole des Beaux-Arts in Aix

1861 Arrives in Paris, frequents the Académie Suisse, meets Camille Pissarro and Armand Guillaumin. Returns to Aix in September and starts work in his father's bank

1862 Leaves bank in January and devotes himself entirely to painting. In November, goes to Paris for the second time

1863 Lives in Paris and works at the Académie Suisse. He and Émile Zola visit the Salon and Salon des Refusés

1866 The jury of the Salon rejects his *Portrait of Valabrègue*. Cézanne writes a letter of protest to Count Nieuwerkerke, superintendent of the Beaux-Arts, with the demand that the Salon des Refusés be reopened. Zola writes a series of articles in defense of avant-garde artists in the newspaper *L'Événement* and publishes them in a separate pamphlet with a dedication to Cézanne

1872 Birth of Paul, the son of Hortense Fiquet. Cézanne lives in Pontoise and Auvers-sur-Oise, where he works with Pissarro

1874 Takes part in the first Impressionist exhibition (the "Société anonyme des artistes peintres, sculpteurs et graveurs"), held from April 15 through May 15

1877 Works with Pissarro at Auvers and Pontoise. Participates in the third Impressionist exhibition

1882 Works with Auguste Renoir at L'Estaque. For the first time is admitted to the Salon as "a pupil of Guillemet"

1886 Cézanne's father dies, leaving him a sizable legacy

1888 In January, Renoir comes to work with Cézanne at Aix

1890 Exhibits three paintings at the seventh exhibition of "*Les XX*" in Brussels

1895 First one-man exhibition at Ambroise Vollard's on Rue Laffitte. Gustave Geffroy writes an article about the exhibition

1898 Exhibition at the Salon des Indépendants. Cézanne's exhibition organized by Vollard

1901 Maurice Denis exhibits *Homage to Cézanne* at the Salon of the Société des Artistes Français

1902 Builds a studio at Chemin des Lauves not far from Aix. Exhibits two works at the Société des Amis des Arts in Aix

1903 Takes part in the Impressionist exhibition at the Vienna Secession

1904 Contributes works to the Impressionist exhibition sponsored by the Société de la Libre Esthétique in Brussels. Émile Bernard visits Cézanne in Aix and writes a major article about him in the review *L'Occident*

1905 Exhibits at the Salon d'Automne and the Salon des Indépendants. Bernard, Denis, and Roussel visit Cézanne

1906 *View of the Château Noir* exhibited at the Société des Amis des Arts in Aix as the work of one of Pissarro's pupils. Dies on October 22

1. TWO WOMEN AND CHILD IN AN INTERIOR. Early 1860s
Oil on canvas. $35^{3}/_{4} \times 28^{1}/_{4}''$ (91 $\times$ 72 cm)
The Pushkin Museum of Fine Arts, Moscow

2. GIRL AT THE PIANO. OVERTURE TO TANNHÄUSER. 1868—69
Oil on canvas. $22^1/_2 \times 36^1/_4''$ (57×92 cm)
The Hermitage, Leningrad

3. ROAD AT PONTOISE. 1878

Oil on canvas. $22^7/_8 \times 27''$ (58 $\times$ 71 cm)

The Pushkin Museum of Fine Arts, Moscow

4. SELF-PORTRAIT. 1879—85
Oil on canvas. 17³/₄ × 14³/₄″ (45 × 37 cm)
The Pushkin Museum of Fine Arts, Moscow

6. THE BANKS OF THE MARNE. c. 1888
Oil on canvas. 27 × 35$^1/_8$″ (71 × 90 cm)
The Pushkin Museum of Fine Arts, Moscow

7. PIERROT AND HARLEQUIN. MARDI GRAS. 1888

Oil on canvas. $40^1/_8 \times 31^7/_8''$ (102 × 81 cm)

The Pushkin Museum of Fine Arts, Moscow

8. PEACHES AND PEARS. 1888—90
Oil on canvas. 24 × 35$^1/_8$" (61 × 90 cm)
The Pushkin Museum of Fine Arts, Moscow

9. BATHERS. Study. Early 1890s
Oil on canvas. $10^{1}/_{4} \times 15^{3}/_{4}''$ (26 × 40 cm)
The Pushkin Museum of Fine Arts, Moscow

10. GREAT PINE NEAR AIX. Late 1890s
Oil on canvas. $28^{1}/_{4} \times 35^{3}/_{4}''$ (72×91 cm)
The Hermitage, Leningrad

11. THE SMOKER. 1895—1900
Oil on canvas. $35^3/_4 \times 28^1/_4''$ (91×72 cm)
The Hermitage, Leningrad

12. STILL LIFE WITH CURTAIN. 1899
Oil on canvas. 20³/₄ × 28¹/₄″ (53 × 72 cm)
The Hermitage, Leningrad

13. MONT SAINTE-VICTOIRE. 1896—98
Oil on canvas. $30^3/_4 \times 39''$ (78 $\times$ 99 cm)
The Hermitage, Leningrad

14. LADY IN BLUE. 1904

Oil on canvas. 35 × 28¹/₄″ (88.5 × 72 cm)
The Hermitage, Leningrad

15. THE BLUE LANDSCAPE. 1904—6
Oil on canvas. $40^1/_8 \times 32^3/_4''$ (102 $\times$ 83 cm)
The Hermitage, Leningrad

16. LANDSCAPE AT AIX (MONT SAINTE-VICTOIRE). 1905—6
Oil on canvas. $23^{1}/_{4} \times 28^{3}/_{4}$" ($60 \times 73$ cm)
The Pushkin Museum of Fine Arts, Moscow

ПОЛЬ СЕЗАНН

Альбом (на английском языке)

ИЗДАТЕЛЬСТВО „АВРОРА". ЛЕНИНГРАД. 1981

Изд. № 3268

Типография имени Ивана Федорова, Ленинград

Printed and bound in the USSR